We Remember the Day of President Kennedy's Assassination

John F. Kennedy Motorcade, Dallas, TX, Nov. 22, 1963

We Remember the Day of President Kennedy's Assassination

November 22, 1963

Barbara O'Shea

William R. Parks

W. R. PARKS

Hershey, PA

Published by William R. Parks
Hershey, Pennsylvania

E-mail: **wparkspublishing (at) aol.com**
Web Site: **www.wrparks.com**
Twitter: **www.twitter.com/wparkspublishing**
Facebook: **www.facebook.com/wparkspublishing**

ACKNOWLEDGEMENTS

We would like to express our deep appreciation to the many people who recollected, wrote and emailed their memories of President John F. Kennedy's assassination. We included their provided names, occupations, and places of residence on the day of the assassination.

Special thanks to historian, Arthur Parks, for his very informative Foreword and Appendix which contain information not mentioned elsewhere.

TABLE OF CONTENTS

FOREWORD

As I write this in 2017, it is interesting to realize that if President John F. Kennedy were still alive, he would be celebrating his 100th birthday on May 29. He was born less than two months after the United States entered World War I by declaring war against Germany and its allies in April 1917.

This book is based on memory: do you remember the impact the assassination of President John F. Kennedy had on you on a day 54 years prior to 2017? Obviously, respondents to this question must be seniors at least sixty years old. Quite a challenge for one's memory; however, was John F. Kennedy a remarkable man worthy of exploring a half-century memory bank? My answer to this question is based on a life-long study of American history and is a definite yes!

The following are accurate descriptive adjectives, which are honest appraisals of him: charismatic, brave, jovial, intelligent, inspiring, self-reliant and electrifying. Kennedy is worthy of being remembered not only because of his brilliant but short Presidency but also because of his accomplishments as a young man prior to his service as President. The following is a timeline that provides justification for this collection of memories!

1917—born in Brookline, Massachusetts on May 29
1922-1935—attended elite private schools such as Choate School in Connecticut
1935—attended London School of Economics, England

1936—attended Harvard University, Cambridge, Massachusetts

1940—published his first book, Why England Slept, which was highly praised and discussed

1941—received a commission as Ensign in the U.S. Navy on October 5

1942—sent to the PT Boat Training School of the U.S. Navy

1943—was given command of PT Boat 109 in the Solomon Islands, South Pacific, with the rank of Lieutenant, Junior Grade in March

1943—PT 109 was rammed and sunk by a Japanese destroyer killing two crewmen on August 2. Kennedy inspired the survivors to swim for four hours to an island while towing an injured crewman by his life preserver straps. Friendly natives carried a message carved on a coconut shell to an Australian military station, which sent a rescue team for Kennedy and his crew. Kennedy was awarded the following for his heroism and leadership: the Marine Medal, the Navy Medal and the Purple Heart.

1943—returned to the U.S. in December and was hospitalized for malaria and injuries

1944—underwent disc surgery in the Naval Hospital, Boston

1945—received an Honorable Discharge from the Navy

1945—authored a memorial tribute to his brother, Joseph, who was killed as a naval pilot in Europe during World War II.

1945—served as a reporter for the International News Service covering the birth of the United Nations in San Francisco

1946—elected to the U.S. House of Representatives in November and sworn in on January 3, 1947 He was re-elected twice more for the 81st and 82nd Congress.

1952—elected Senator from Massachusetts by defeating Senator Henry C. Lodge in November and sworn in on January 3, 1953.

1953—married Jacqueline L. Bouvier in Newport, Rhode Island on September 12

1954 & 1955—underwent two surgeries on his spinal column in October and February

1956—wrote Profiles in Courage, which was published by Harper. The book became a best-seller and won the Pulitzer Prize for Biography in 1957.

1956—became an unsuccessful candidate for U.S. Vice President at the Democratic National Convention in Chicago

1958—reelected to the U.S. Senate in November

1960—nominated for the U.S. President at the Democratic National Convention on the first ballot in July in Los Angeles

1960—won the popular vote on November 8, 1960, by a narrow margin: Kennedy 34.2 million and Nixon 34.1 million votes. When the electoral votes were cast in December, Kennedy received 303 votes; Nixon received 219 votes; Harry Byrd received 15 votes.

1961—was sworn in office as the 35th president of the U.S. on January 20, 1961, by Chief Justice Earl Warren. He donated his salary to charity.

1961—gave the first live presidential news conference in history on January 25 with over sixty million viewers

1961—sent a large number of recommendations to Congress in February that include these examples:

     —increase the benefit in Social Security
     —extend unemployment benefits
     —boost minimum hourly wage
     —provide financial help to Cuban refugees
     —promote foreign travel in the U.S.

—set up a health insurance program for the aged

—set up a scholarship program for college students going into medical fields

1961—created the Peace Corps Program in March and appointed Sargent Shriver as its Director

1961—publicly took responsibility for the "Bay of Pigs" failure in April

1961—strongly promoted manned space exploration

1961—visited European nations such as France, Italy, England, Austria

1961—visited South American nations such as Venezuela and Columbia in December

1962—proposed welfare reform and fiscal aid to public schools in February

1962—ordered the military quarantine of Cuba during the Missile Crisis and nuclear confrontation with the USSR in October. The Russians under Khrushchev agreed to dismantle and remove missile bases in Cuba.

1963—visited Germany and West Berlin where he made his famous Ich Bin Ein Berliner (I am a Berliner) speech to a crowd of one million in protest to Communist attempts to isolate Berlin by building the infamous Berlin Wall.

1963—shot by Lee Harvey Oswald on November 22 in Dallas while riding in a motorcade   —1:00 p.m. CST was the official time of death noted by the medical staff of Parkland Hospital. (N.B. Oswald was shot and killed on November 24 in the Municipal Building by Jack Ruby [Rubenstein], a nightclub owner.)

Most people remember his stirring Inaugural Address that included these profound messages for all time: "Now the trumpet summons us again—not as a call to bear arms, though arms we need—not as a call to battle, though embattled we are—but a call to bear the burden of a long twilight struggle, year in and year out, 'rejoicing in hope, patient in tribulation' —a struggle against the common enemies of man: tyranny, poverty, disease and war itself… And so, my fellow Americans: ask not what your country can do for you—ask what you can do for your country."

Arthur Parks

B.A. Cum Laude, American History, Grove City College

M.A. American History, University of Notre Dame

PREFACE

Newspaper reporters, TV and radio announcers were in agreement when they stated that people all over the world will remember what that they were doing on the day President John F. Kennedy was assassinated. This book is a collection of people's memories.

What circumstances prevailed in your life on the day President John F. Kennedy was assassinated in Dallas, Texas, Friday, November 22, 1963 and died of gunshot wounds fired by his assassin, Lee Harvey Oswald?

Although millions of viewers witnessed the assassination of Lee Harvey Oswald, as well, and memorable events of the next few days, no one can forget the poignant moment in television news broadcasting when Walter Cronkite, choked up and stifled with grief, uncharacteristically removed his glasses and began speaking to the nation and the rest of the world, hesitantly confirming the shocking reality that "President John F. Kennedy was pronounced dead at one o'clock p.m. Central Standard Time."

According to experts in the field of psychology of learning, it seems clear that, as a basic rule, emotionally charged experiences are more easily remembered. This is especially true if the event is something we want to remember. So we ask, is what happened in our lives on the day President Kennedy was assassinated something we want to remember? Yes, of course it is! It is something we never want to forget. It should live in infamy like the Japanese attack on Pearl Harbor on December 7, 1941. We learn from these tragic events and continue to strive for world peace.

W.R. Klemm, Texas A&M University, neuroscience writer and professor, agrees that memory is bolstered and reinforced by dramatic circumstances. We, therefore, are more likely to remember what happened in our lives on the day President Kennedy died, the terrorist attack on the World Trade Center, Columbine High School shootings, and Oklahoma Federal Building bombing.

We decided to go out and ask people to tell us what they remember about the day John F. Kennedy was assassinated. We were not surprised at how easily they could relate to this topic and submit their responses to us in writing. In doing so, all those who dedicated their time and effort to this work have shared with us in commemorating the 35th President of the United States as we celebrate the 100th anniversary of his birth.

Barbara O'Shea   **William Parks**

We Remember the Day of President Kennedy's Assassination

November 22, 1963; Location: Dealey Plaza, Dallas,
Texas, U.S.A. Minutes before the assassination of
President John F. Kennedy riding in a limousine on
Main Street. In the presidential limousine with
Kennedy are his wife, Jackie Kennedy, Texas
Governor John Connally, and his wife, Nellie.

Polaroid photograph of the assassination of President John F. Kennedy, taken one-sixth of a second after the fatal head shot. Mrs. Kennedy can be seen reacting in desperation and grasping her husband's shoulders.

Two hours after the assassination Lyndon B. Johnson took the oath of office aboard Air Force One at Love Field Airport in Dallas, Texas. Lady Bird Johnson and former First Lady Jackie Kennedy with blood-soaked clothes, look on.

Jack Ruby shot Lee Harvey Oswald as he was being transferred by police to the Dallas County jail, Sunday, November 24, 1963. Oswald was escorted by police detectives Jim Leavelle (in the light tan suit) and L.C. Graves.

Marjorie Meyers – Retired Nurses' Aide

It was Friday, November 22, 1963. I was living in Alden, New York and had no plans for that day. It was going to be a nice relaxing day. I seated myself comfortably in my front room in time to watch the motorcade of our president on television from Dallas, Texas.

All of a sudden, I saw our president, John F. Kennedy slumped over in the back seat of an open convertible car in which he was riding. He was seated next to his wife, Jackie who jumped up in panic. I was so confused and shocked by what I was watching. I couldn't help but cry as the news unfolded. I didn't want to believe our president had been assassinated. This kind of thing couldn't happen to us.

I was in disbelief. I had felt so safe before this; the thought of this occurring had never even crossed my mind. I still vividly remember the action of the first lady, Jackie, jumping up in a panic trying to save her own life after realizing her husband had been shot. That memory is something I will always remember. I kept the newspaper from that day to look back on. That day was so significant in our country's history.

Michael J. Butler – Bronx, NY

Fifty-four years can erode memories, but I do recall some distinct images and feelings from that late-fall day when John F. Kennedy was assassinated.

Sitting in my 3rd grade classroom at Holy Rosary Catholic Grammar School in the Bronx, New York, I remember being snapped out of my usual mid-day lethargy by an announcement from our principal, Sister Dorothy.

"Children, please bow your heads and pray. The president of the United States has been shot." In unison, twenty-five plus boys and girls silently placed their heads on their respective desks. I remember closing my eyes and drifting into a quiet somber rest. Not feeling particularly shocked or grief-stricken, I was enveloped in the same solitude that gripped the entire class.

I did not anticipate another announcement, but shortly after (less than a half-hour it seemed), Sister Dorothy's voice, now even more shaken, emerged from the P.A. system.

"Children, please bow your heads and pray. The president is dead." A pall of silence surrounded us as we prayed silently for our president. Normally, a lively classroom, it almost had the quiet and reverence of Church. That quiet, sad, solemn feeling is what I remember most.

My next recollection is Lee Harvey Oswald being shot and killed. I sat watching our small 19" black and white TV in the living room, waiting for our usual Sunday dinner to be served. My mother was hovering over a large pot of tomato sauce, meatballs, and sausage in the kitchen. I could smell the aroma of garlic, basil, and tomato sauce and was looking forward to stealing a meatball or two before the large pasta dinner was served.

Suddenly, a news-flash covered the TV screen. A picture of Lee Harvey Oswald, doubled over, was shown over and over. I am not sure how much time elapsed, but he was pronounced dead. I remember thinking—*Good, he deserved to die for killing the president.*

The day of the President's funeral we were given off from school. A bunch of us boys gathered in the park hoping to get a football game going. For some reason, whether it was out of respect, guilt, or sadness, we never did play that game.

.

Herman Daniel Sturm – Air-traffic Controller – Madrid, Spain

I was in the United States Air Force stationed at Torrejon Air Force base located 20 miles northeast of Madrid, Spain. I was celebrating my 21st birthday with a group of my fellow Air Force men at a favorite bar in downtown Madrid. It was about 8 pm when we overheard some of the Spanish people in the bar exclaiming in Spanish, "*Presidente Kennedy esta muerte!*" (President Kennedy is dead!) and that he had been shot. My fellow Air Force men and I knew we needed to contact our base immediately to find out what to do.

So, we hurried outside and hopped on the bus for the long ride that took us back to the base. We sat quietly in total disbelief wondering how and why this could happen. When we arrived back at Torrejon, we were informed that the base was on Emergency Alert status, and everyone was instructed to return to the base at once. In fact, we were restricted from leaving the base for about two weeks for security reasons until most details of the assassination were known and things had settled down.

All of us had access to radios of our own, so we could keep up with the news. Local stations, however, were broadcast in Spanish. But we listened to radio broadcasts throughout Europe from a station off base. During the days following the assassination, our work in the Air Force continued. I worked in air-traffic control and reported every day. I don't recall any Memorial Service for the president, but his funeral was televised worldwide.

Stars and Stripes, a military newspaper was printed in English and was available for all of us to read. So, we were able to keep up with the news from back home in the states as it unfolded.

Jim Taylor – Home Inspector – Binghamton, NY

I was an 8th grade student at Saint Paul's Catholic School in Binghamton, NY on November 22, 1963. Saint Paul's was K-8th grade, so I was a senior, so to speak. Our school was back-to-back with a Binghamton public grade school, Thomas Edison.

We did not have TV's or radios at our school and had no idea what news was shaking the earth as we knew it. It so happened that I was tasked with carrying a note of some sort across the parking lot and through the chain link gate to the Thomas Edison office. I never learned what was in that note.

The news had reached Thomas Edison, and I carried the sadness on my shoulders back to my teacher at Saint Paul's. Once the good Sisters of Saint Joseph of Carondelet gathered radios from the convent and the news was absorbed to whatever degree possible, classes were dismissed, and we students were sent home.

The walk home was short, but it seemed to take forever. The rest of the day we were consumed by unending newsreels and the voice of Walter Cronkite. We lived upstairs from my cherished grandfather. I sat with him watching the tragedy unfold over and over.

Sadly for me, and I can only assume most of America, this was a coarse introduction to the world of modern communications. Never again would the news be served up at 6 p.m. only, as if that were the only time of day that it mattered.

As a thirteen year old, news hadn't mattered much before. Now there was this nightmare to deal with. The tears I shed at 13 were destined to erupt twice again less than five years later, with the shock of the assassination of Martin Luther King, Jr. in April, 1968 and JFK's younger brother Robert F. Kennedy two months later in June.

How many times must we repeat? Never again!

Carol Haber – Retired Teacher – Oneonta, NY

We were living in Oneonta, New York. Upon returning home from a walk outside on this cold but sunny afternoon, as usual, I turned on the television at 1:35 p.m. to watch "As the World Turns".

What I saw instead to my amazement was Walter Cronkite announcing that President John F. Kennedy had just been shot in Dallas, Texas. I remember putting Patrick (6 mos. old) in the playpen still in his snowsuit.

It was Alumni Weekend at SUNY Oneonta, but the Alumni basketball game, and all activities would all be cancelled. Our friends from Long Island arrived at our house at four o'clock that afternoon and had planned to enjoy the weekend events with us but instead would return home the next morning.

At five o'clock, while watching the news on TV, they showed a reel of JFK speaking at a past event. Gary, (3 ½ years old), started yelling, "He's not dead! He's talking!"

It was very sad and shocking for my parents, as well. In fact, later that evening, my mother called from Binghamton, New York. She thought my dad, who had a history of asthma and emphysema, was dying, as he was suddenly having great difficulty breathing and was being taken to the Our Lady of Lourdes Hospital.

We left for Binghamton early the next morning. Dad was already in surgery having a tracheotomy when we arrived. My husband returned home on Sunday, but the boys and I stayed the entire week. Dad lived almost four years after the tracheotomy.

Therese Clarke – Educator – Buffalo, NY

I was a young Junior High School teacher in a suburb of Buffalo, New York. It was during the change of classes when the announcement was made on the school's public address system informing everyone that President John Kennedy had been shot. Our school hallways were, therefore, crowded with boisterous young people on the way to class. We learned that the president was riding in an open car that was part of a motorcade in Dallas, Texas. It was further explained on the public address system that word of the president's condition would be forthcoming, after he had been examined by doctors at Parkland Hospital.

Everyone was, of course, stunned by the news. Some of the children remained silent, while others were shoving and shouting. I don't remember the exact words because I was trying to absorb the news and also thinking about my next class and how I would deal with the situation. I remember hearing shouts like, "Hooray!", "Hope he dies", which were cruel and hurt me to the core. It was heartbreaking to hear that and to think that immature students were prone to shouting horrible words, just as they would often poke fun at their classmates. It was Friday, so the weekend would help everyone digest the news.

Later, at home with my parents, Walter Cronkite's brief, emotional announcement that our president had succumbed to his injuries was broadcast. The realization that President Kennedy had been brutally and purposefully assassinated shocked the entire country as well as most of the world.

It seemed to me that time stood still as the country was absorbed in media coverage non-stop for a few days. As details emerged about the incident, and plans for a period of mourning and a state funeral unfolded, we watched attentively. I would say I was "glued" to the television for the entire four days!

I remember that all day and night hundreds of thousands of mourners, many openly weeping, filed by the coffin which was under the dome of the U.S. Capitol. I remember watching the funeral procession and the horse-drawn caisson and one of the horses having no rider. Jackie was standing with the crowds lining the streets. Little John-John, in a pale blue coat, stood at attention and saluted as the caisson passed by.

The images of Jackie dressed in the pink suit she wore during the motorcade in Dallas the day of the assassination, and now that same blood-stained suit she steadfastly wore for the rest of that fateful day, remain unforgettable. When I think back on this singular event, other images of the first family come flooding back: little John-John crawling under the desk in the Oval Office, and Jackie and the television special of her tour of the White House.

Since that day, I have traveled to Dallas with my daughter. We visited Dealey Plaza and the Texas Book Depository, part of which is now a museum located on the sixth floor. It remains quite a tourist attraction.

J.M.P. – Retired – Dunkirk, NY

My husband Bill and I were living in a house on the corner of Pangolin and Lakefront Streets in Dunkirk, NY. We had been married in July and I was experiencing pregnancy related *morning sickness* that November. I was home alone that day.

The kitchen radio was on and I heard a news bulletin saying that President Kennedy had been hit by a bullet in Texas. I assumed he had been in a hunting accident on Lyndon Johnson's ranch.

I can't remember what caused me to turn on the television in the living room. Perhaps, Bill or someone else called to tell me there was news coverage. I watched Walter Cronkite. I saw and heard his announcement, President Kennedy was dead.

Later that day, Bill, his brother Joe and I went to a diner that was part of Rusch's Restaurant on Lake Shore Drive. The place was almost empty. We sat in a booth and we were numb with shock. Then I heard a waitress behind the counter laughing about something. Laughter on this sad day was inappropriate.

As the weekend events were covered on television, we watched with interest and sadness. My *morning sickness* had vanished.

Richard J. Lutz

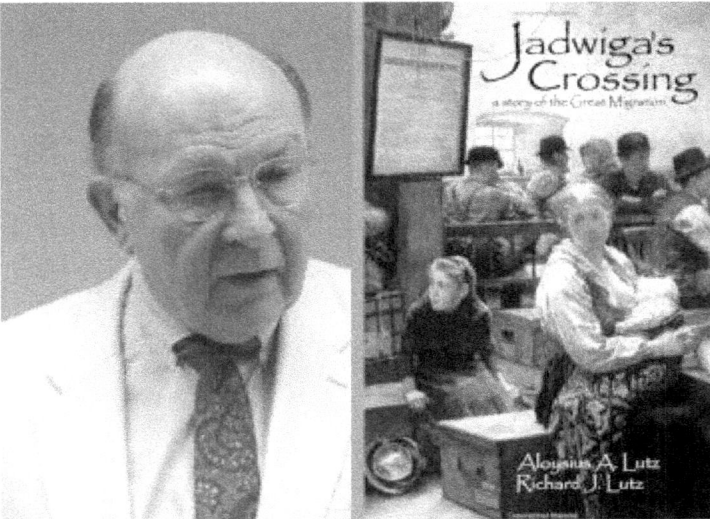

Richard J. Lutz has retired after a career that ranged across print media, broadcasting, and the advent of the Internet and the World Wide Web. He is the author, with his father, of *Jadwiga's Crossing* (available on Amazon.com), an historical novel of Polish migration to the United States. A sequel, *Jadwiga's America*, will be published for Christmas, 2017. DickLutz@usa.net.

I was in graduate school at The University of Michigan in 1963 and I had part-time jobs on the campus. On 11/22/63 I was in my office at The University of Michigan Television Center (UMTV), where I worked on publicity for the educational productions the Center provided (as kinescope recordings – remember those, TV veterans?) to stations that needed "product" to run in fringe time, just after morning sign-on.

In those days, stations signed on around 5:00 or 6:00 a.m., and signed off – with the *Star-Spangled Banner* as accompaniment to various demonstrations of military strength – around 11:30 or midnight. My favorite rendering of the national anthem was a maneuvering jet with a deep male voice interpreting John Gillespie Magee, Jr.'s *High Flight*. The last lines:

> "And, while with silent, lifting mind I've trod
> The high untrespassed sanctity of space,
> Put out my hand, and touched the face of God."

It was a time of unity and patriotism in America – a time when every American could respect our leader and love the opposition (who could resist Everett Dirkson – "...a million here, a million there, and pretty soon, you're talking real money.")

On November 22, in the UMTV graphics studio, a TV set was tuned to the CBS station in Detroit. I happened to pass by as a "News Bulletin" slide gave way and Walter Cronkite told the nation that, in Dallas, shots had been fired at the President's motorcade. I uttered an expletive, but went back to work, thinking that "shots fired" was the whole story. An assassination was unthinkable.

The venerable Director of Broadcasting at the university, Garnet Garrison, had a decision to make. One of the networks was to broadcast a U-M football game on Saturday, and they had rented UMTV equipment to complement their mobile facility. The question: Would the football game happen, or be canceled, and should the technical staff start delivering equipment to the press box at the stadium?

Garrison was one of my personal heros, and I felt privileged that he talked the matter over with me. Initially, he planned to go ahead with the equipment delivery, but he thought it over aloud: "When FDR died," he said, "everything stopped." That clinched the decision.

I was an unabashed JFK fan. His murder brought feelings of despair, but I was headed for a career in television, so I also planned to pay close attention to the coverage on all three networks. That meant that I saw Lee Harvey Oswald fall to Jack Ruby's pistol shot, John-John's proud salute, and the lighting of the eternal flame. My patriotic feelings surged, and I felt great pride in the industry I was about to join: Television unifed the country at a time when there were three choices of local station, plus, perhaps, an "educational station."

Exactly one year later, on November 22, 1964, transmissions started from WITF-TV in Hershey, Pennsylvania, and I was there as Program Manager. The first program we aired was a documentary on the terrible events of one year earlier.

The feelings surged again, but this time, there was no need to worry over our democracy and the succession of presidential power. We knew: The *best* among us would rise to power.

Dr. Gerry Rising – Author – SUNY Distinguished Teaching Professor Emeritus

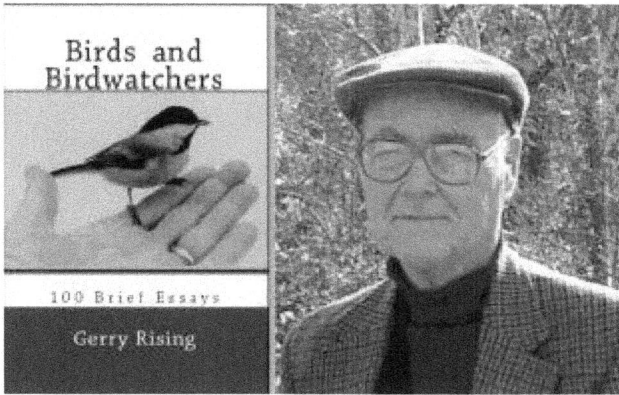

On the day John Kennedy was shot I was working as mathematics coordinator for the Norwalk, Connecticut schools. I don't know who first learned of the shooting, but almost immediately the word spread through our administration building in the city center. The response I recall was universal shock. Both men and women were in tears.

I remember in particular that there was no distinction in their reaction by political party affiliation. One of my close friends who had strongly opposed Kennedy during the election was as deeply disturbed as were Kennedy supporters.

There was no announcement but all group work came to a halt. My colleagues and I wanted either privacy or association in small groups of close personal friends.

It was a very sad day.

Charles P. Pisano

**Charles touring downtown Frankfort Germany
during 39 months at Rhein Main Air Force Base,
which was part of the occupation forces.**

I did not pay much attention to politics until John F. Kennedy ran for President of the United States. I was attending King's College, a Catholic men's school in Wilkes-Barre, Pennsylvania at the time. I was very aware of the concern among many that a Catholic would become our President. Perhaps, this is the reason I became so interested in the election.

I recall lying in bed into the wee hours of the night listening to the election results on the radio. I did not know Kennedy had won until I got up the next morning. It was a good feeling!

Shortly after I graduated from King's College, I got a job at a U.S Navy Facility in Central Pennsylvania. I was at work when President Kennedy was assassinated on November 22, 1963. There were no TV's, cell phones or iPhones to alert us to what had happened.

The office telephones started ringing. Spouses calling spouses, friends calling friends, contacts calling contacts. People were running through the aisles calling out, "The President has been shot, the President has been shot!"

I stepped into a nearby room where some people were busy working. I told them what I had just heard. Some got angry with me and said, "Hey, that's not funny!"

By the end of the work day, the phones stopped ringing, people stopped talking, and many left the facility early. It was like a morgue.

Michelle Claus – Retired Teacher – Tonawanda, NY

Michelle ready for semi-formal school dance

My life as an eighth grader was, I remember, normal. I attended a junior high school in Tonawanda, New York. My girlfriends and I were silly twelve-year-olds. I can't remember why, but we called ourselves the "seven gazans."

My parents had jobs that had us cared for by only one of them during the week. My father was a salesman, and my mother was a nurse. She worked the night shift and slept while we were at school. The days at school were filled with silliness. My favorite class for silliness was Mr. Cadwell's science class. We laughed and had long necklaces that we draped over each other during class when time allowed.

I remember the day. I remember the time. I remember how everything changed. The day started with my friends and I planning to go to another friend's house after school to snack and play card games. We planned the "fun" for science class, too. We quickly took our seats and began our silly fun. All of a sudden, our principal came over the loudspeaker—so unusual. We immediately turned our heads toward the speaker. Our president had been shot and died. Mr. Cadwell was so upset. We watched a movie for the rest of the class time. Everyone was quiet and sad—no silliness! We were dismissed at the end of the school day.

I could hardly wait to get home. I needed my mom. I walked into her bedroom. Yes, she was sleeping. I sat down next to her on the bed. I touched her and tried to wake her. "Chelle, why are you waking me?" she asked. I told her that President Kennedy had been shot. She started crying and saying, "No, no, no!" I tried to comfort her, but she got up and turned on the TV. Yes, the President was dead! She cried harder, and so did I, mainly for the heartache my mother was experiencing. We hugged each other and talked about the news on TV.

We were sad and waited for my dad to call that evening. He was out of town at a sales meeting. My dad cried, too. I will never forget our family's pain for our President and the Kennedy family, as well.

E.T.A. – Foreign Service in Belgrade, Yugoslavia

**Driving to border in a
land rover to witness
opening of border between
Yugoslavia and Bulgaria.**

**Kalemegdan Fortress
Belgrade**

My husband was a Foreign Service Officer and our first assignment was in Belgrade. At the time, Josef Broz Tito was President of the then Yugoslavia. A Serbian friend, Jelena, telephoned me the evening of November 22nd around 7:00 p.m. Belgrade time to tell me that the President had been shot. Stunned, I told her how sorry I was and concerned for the future of her country and if there was anything I could do to help her through the next few days which I thought might be difficult, please let me know. She then realized that I thought it was Tito who had been assassinated and she exclaimed that no, no - it was President Kennedy who had died. There was a long, long silence and then we both cried.

We didn't have a television there but did have a huge Grundig console which included a short-wave radio, so I turned to the BBC and listened. I think we listened all night long.

Jim McConkey – A Black Day for Mankind – Washington, DC

Jim wrote a 342 page book about his Peace Corps Memoirs

Jim McConkey in 1963

That terrible November 22, I was at family friend Joe Colgan's DuPont Circle apartment in Washington, D.C. The phone rang. "This is not People's Drug Store," Joe muttered, lifting the receiver. Callers had been dialing his number trying to reach People's, and he was fed up with it. Joe was making a map for one of historian Dale Morgan's pioneer books, Overland in 1846, and had asked if I'd like to help. I was a twenty-year-old journalism student at the George Washington University. Any place I could stick a finger into the publishing world, I would so stick.

"Hello?" Joe answered the phone. "Yes, I have. It's lovely."

Then I heard him say: "What?"

"Who shot him?"

"Oh, my God. We're going from bad to worse."

He motioned me to the phone . It was my mother . President Kennedy had been shot. I think she was crying. There was an unconfirmed report that he was dead.

Joe poured a drink. "Pour me one, too."

Dismay, fury, confusion, mixed up in a cocktail shaker. I tried doing a little lettering on the map, but my hand shook too badly.

My mother called back—Kennedy was dead.

I went looking for a paper, but none was out yet. We decided to find a radio and walked to the Embassy Steak House, just above the Circle on Connecticut Avenue. Joe ordered a martini, asked if I wanted wine. " I'll have a martini, too."

The news reports came every five minutes, but nothing could undo the horrible fact.

I got restless and told Joe I had to get to school. I walked back toward his apartment, headed up New Hampshire Avenue instead of out P Street, and walked all the way to Q before realizing I wasn't where I was supposed to be.

I ran back to Dupont Circle, walked rapidly to Joe's, picked up my books, and headed toward school.

I'd just crossed L Street when I saw a boy running with an armload of papers—the Washington Daily News. I bought one. The headline covered more than half the front page: "JFK SLAIN IN TEXAS."

I stopped at my Burmese classmate, Binnya Maw's room. He'd been asleep and was shaving. His radio was on, very softly, and I assumed he'd heard the news.

After a barely audible newscast, I said, "What kind of barbarians are we?" He looked at me quizzically, hadn't heard. "The President has been assassinated," I said. He didn't get it. I had to say it three more times and show him the headline.

"Gee-e-e . . ." escaped his mouth. "What? . . . In America? . . . Those days are over. . . . Here? . . . My . . . golly . . . Ken-ne-dy, Ken-ne-dy, Ken-ne-dy," he trailed off echoing the German crowd's chants after the "Ich bin ein Berliner" speech.

"Truly these are black days for all mankind," I wrote to my brother in the army in Germany. "Even Mother Nature seems to know, for her brow is gloomy and she has been weeping profoundly for her hero." It was grey, overcast, and raining.

We moved through the days in a fog. How had this been possible? The three national TV networks did a remarkable thing. From the assassination through the funeral four days later, they didn't run a commercial.

Maria Gutierrez – Retired Teacher

I was living in Union City, New Jersey with my husband and our two children at the time. I had grown up in Cuba and moved to the United States as an adult.

I remember that Friday, November 22, 1963. My husband had gone to work, and I was home with our two children. My son was two-years old at the time and my daughter was just 11 months old. That day had been like many others. I was feeding my daughter when my husband arrived home early to check on us. This seemed very odd.

The phone rang; it was a friend of mine calling from Cuba. She quickly blurted out, " How do you feel that your president is dead!?"

I couldn't believe what she was saying to me; I was shaken up and scared. We didn't have a television set at our house, so we rushed to our neighbor Maureen's house where we watched the news unfold. I couldn't believe it—I thought it had to be a mistake.

I was so saddened by this act, I remembered President Kennedy's inauguration and his promises of all he would do for us—how he would help better our country. The assassination of our president caused me to lose trust in people at the time. Weren't there supposed to be people protecting him? Did they aid in his assassination? I couldn't help but wonder if a conspiracy was the cause.

In the following days, my sadness changed to anger. I became withdrawn. I kept to myself. I had a hard time taking care of my children and lost interest in doing art, which had been one of my favorite activities. Luckily, I had my husband who stayed home to watch our children while a friend took me to the movies in an attempt to get my mind off things.

Dr. Paul Carlson – Retired Veterinarian
Dunkirk, NY

In November of 1963, I was a 15 year old kid in a segregated high school in Forest Park, Georgia. No colored kids were allowed! My younger sister and brother were in integrated schools because of forced integration by the federal government at that time. Racial tensions were high.

My father Neil was very interested in the civil rights movement, more as a psychologist than an activist. He obtained a stipend to get his Master's degree in counseling and psychology from Atlanta University from 1963 to 1964. At that time it was a black university, with very few whites enrolled.

On the day that President Kennedy was shot, the announcement came over the PA system in my school. I was shocked and saddened, but many of my classmates cheered the news! Those were the days of real racism.

I did not decide to become a veterinarian until the following year, after we were back home on the farm in Chautauqua County, NY. Our family certainly got a taste of the cultural divide at the time of JFK's assassination.

Frederick G. Conway – Retired Guidance Counselor
Seaford, Long Island, NY

I will never forget the day that JFK was murdered. It was Friday, November 22, 1963. I was a new teacher in a 7th grade American History class at Seaford Junior-Senior High School in Seaford, Long Island, NY when that awful news came across the public address system.

Everyone in that class and down the hallways reacted as never seen or heard before. It was a devastating most tragic event. It closed the school down. Kids and faculty alike were totally shocked. There was sobbing, crying out and hateful expressions everywhere.

After dismissal, all after-school activities and weekend events were cancelled. Some of the faculty members adjourned to a local establishment to discuss and carry out our amazement in derogatory and fearful dialogue for what may soon happen.

We stayed well into the night watching the horrific details on TV. It was the weekend now, but we wondered how we would be able to go back to our classrooms and teach on Monday.

Fortunately, we soon learned that not only schools, but all state and federal buildings would be closed all of Thanksgiving week.

At the time, I didn't realize what impact this would have on my future.

However, listening and talking with faculty members, students, and parents led me to further studies leading to the MS and PD degrees in counselor education. It led me to further assignments as a guidance counselor at Holy Family High School in South Huntington (now St. Anthony's H.S.) and eventually Miller Place, Long Island.

This event was the most profound experience that changed my life and will live forever in my memory. I still have a hard time believing this all really happened. I'm sure that all details have yet to be surfaced. Historically and tragically, the assassination of President John F. Kennedy lives on to this day!

Barbara Peck Barkley – Retired – Syracuse, NY

We were living in Syracuse, New York at the time, and I was pregnant with our third child. My neighbor came running over to tell me that President Kennedy had been shot! I went over to her apartment, and together we watched throughout the afternoon all that was happening. We simply couldn't believe it! At that point, they couldn't confirm that the president had died, and it wasn't until later that Walter Cronkite made the announcement, and we were still in shock.

Seeing poor Mrs. Kennedy as she stood watching Lyndon B. Johnson sworn in as president, the demeanor of all those people so terribly serious—judging by the look on their faces! We watched the news well into the evening as each announcement was made. Even days later, I was still in shock and disbelief.

I remember our church held a special service the following day. The church was packed, and we all kept saying how terrible and shocking it was! Of course, for days that was all we saw and heard, and the real tragedy and most vivid in my mind was the funeral and watching little John standing there and saluting his father's casket as it passed by. It will be something I will never forget!

Beth Green – Retired Teacher – Pittsburgh, PA

I have only a couple disjointed memories of that particular time in my life regarding this horrific event. I remember sitting in Sister Mary Benignetta's fifth-grade classroom at St. Bartholomew School in Pittsburgh, Pennsylvania. Our principal, Sister Mary Leona, came over the loudspeaker to tell us that our president, John F. Kennedy had just been shot in Dallas, Texas and had died. She then asked the entire student body to pray along as she began reciting the rosary.

After that, I recall seeing television coverage of the events at a few different times—when the plane landed in Washington, DC that night, a little bit of the viewing in the Rotunda of the Capitol, and parts of the funeral. In retrospect, I wonder if I have so few memories of that day and the week following because my parents tried to shield me from the television news broadcasts and the emotions of this tragic loss.

I know that on September 11, 2001, I made a conscious effort not to watch TV coverage when my children were in the room—while my sixteen-year-old seemed able to deal with it, the seven-year old was concerned and frightened, and I didn't want to add to that, so I tried to keep things as normal as possible.

C.S.

It was on November 22, 1963 that the President of the United States, John F. Kennedy was shot and killed in Dallas, Texas. I remember it well. My husband and I were living in Swarthmore, Pennsylvania with my mom. I was an only child, so we lived there with my daughters.

Mom and I were sitting in the living room on that day watching a favorite soap opera, and my two little girls were in the playpen. Quite abruptly taking us by surprise, the program was interrupted with the tragic news that President Kennedy had been shot in Dallas, Texas during a motorcade. He was there with Jacqueline, wife and First Lady campaigning for a second term of office. She was seated next to him in the convertible.

Mom and I both started screaming when we heard the news! My husband, who worked outside the house, called soon afterward saying people were yelling in the streets about it. I just felt so bad for our president and his wife and children. I thought JFK was a great person, man, and president. The world really suffered for that loss.

Cindy Smist – Computer Analyst – Newfane, NY

FOR LIBRARY—Pupils who gave up a day of leisure to earn money for the John F. Kennedy Memorial Library fund place contributions in a Student Council collection box at Newfane Elementary School. Left to right are, Gail Grigg, Cynthia Johnson and Barbara Smith.
(US&J — Dan Dwyer)

    I was sitting in my 5th grade classroom in Newfane, NY on the afternoon of November 22, 1963. There was a loud speaker on the front wall of the room just above the chalkboard, and I remember looking at it and hearing the words, "President Kennedy is dead." Time stood still for me, and I felt as if I had lost someone I knew. This happened on a Friday, and my family and I stayed glued to our black-and-white TV set all day Saturday, as well, to watch the unfolding news about the assassination.

On Sunday morning, we attended services at the First Baptist Church located a block from our house. My mother liked to leave food in the oven while we were gone and upon returning, I loved to open the door to the house and sniff the aroma of our noontime dinner.

On this day, we turned on the TV after coming home, and we immediately witnessed the horror of Lee Harvey Oswald being shot on live television.

The following day, we watched the coverage of the president's casket moving through the streets of Washington, D.C., and we knew we had been changed by the events of that weekend; although it was not clear yet how.

On June 5, 1964, I appeared in a photo in the Lockport Union-Sun & Journal promoting our Newfane Elementary School's "Kennedy Project" to raise money for the John F. Kennedy Memorial Library to be built in Massachusetts. Students needed to perform a day of service; then bring in a note detailing what they did, along with a donation. The newspaper article reported that our Student Council, led by Billy Smist, was heading up the fundraiser. I did not know Bill at this time, but I ended up marrying him many years later.

Dennis Priore – Retired Middle School Principal, Kenmore-Town of Tonawanda UFSD, and Current Board of Education Member
Clarence Central School, Clarence, NY

Dennis is sitting at the table.

It was Friday, November 22, 1963. I was a student at Public School #64 located at Amherst and Lincoln Parkway in the City of Buffalo, New York. My third-grade classmates and I were in an art class taught by Miss Emma Lang. Midway through the class, a teacher—whose name I don't recall—burst into our room yelling, "The President has been shot!" At that point Miss Lang yelled, "Oh my God!" and asked for more details but the teacher said she didn't have any.

A short while later, the same teacher stuck her head in our room again and yelled—before walking away crying—"The President is dead!" Our class consisted of groups of four students sitting in clusters of four desks, and I remember one boy who was sitting at my cluster saying, "Oh, good! Now at least he won't interrupt my Saturday morning cartoons anymore." The girl next to me in that cluster said, "That's cruel."

Later that night, my dad drove me over to my aunt Mary (his sister's) house. As she opened the door, the first thing she said was, "Isn't this terrible?" We stayed for a while and watched the coverage on television with Aunt Mary and Uncle Frank.

On Sunday morning two days later, I vividly remember watching on live TV as Dallas Nightclub owner, Jack Ruby shot and killed Lee Harvey Oswald, Kennedy's alleged assassin, while in the process of being transferred in Police Custody to the Dallas County jail at the time.

E.W

I remember it was Friday, November 22, 1963, and I was on parole by myself that day in Philadelphia. I worked for the Police Department. I always carried an FM radio to keep in contact with the police headquarters radio, so I heard the dreadful news of President Kennedy's assassination on my radio.

This alarming news caused a complete state of confusion for the force because we had never experienced anything like it in our lifetime. We had to wait to see if there were any special orders coming down from our supervisor.

I was surprised by this horrific event because to me JFK was doing a decent job. I couldn't see any problem where he was way out of line. He made good decisions and some bad decisions, of course, but he was generally well liked.

Of course, everyone wondered. Was there a plot to take over? Was there a conspiracy? It crossed my mind very quickly and was the topic of conversation, but everyone had different opinions. No one knew at the time, but they had their ideas. The strongest theory that I came across was the mafia.

Once the facts started coming out, the public eventually had a better understanding of the entire account of Kennedy's motorcade through the streets of Dallas; how Oswald entered the picture; then how Ruby came into it and decided to take things into his own hands and get rid of Oswald. The entire investigation and account of the facts weren't really resolved until many years later.

Carol Swica Fisk – Retired Teacher – Dunkirk, NY

I was living in Dunkirk, NY at the time, having just returned from Mesa, Arizona in January of 1963, after living there for a year and half. I was twenty-four years old and had two little boys.

We lived in an upstairs apartment on Franklin Ave. and Doughty Street. I remember the cold, frosty, snowy days of winter as I traveled to Falconer every day to teach third grade.

After that summer of 1963, I was hired at Silver Creek Central School teaching the sixth grade. I remember November 22nd quite clearly. The day started out as any other. Arriving at school, getting ready for the day's lessons, and preparing some notes on the board for a Social Studies class.

Right after lunch, I went to the office to see if I had any notes, etc. to send home with the kids that day. The office secretary told me what had just happened! John F. Kennedy was assassinated while riding in a car in Dallas. We all shed some tears because we felt we lost an outstanding and well-liked President. He was young and seemed able to relate his ideas and platform to the masses. As a tribute to him, I immediately put together a bulletin board in the main hallway of the school. (It was lunch recess, and I had some free time without the children.) When classes resumed for the afternoon, of course we discussed the incident in class.

When I arrived at home, I turned on the TV and watched Walter Cronkite and the news all evening long! I was devastated, as were many others. It was difficult to watch because it was so unexpected on that beautiful sunny day in Texas. I guess everyone has enemies, but, you don't expect it to happen. I spent the whole weekend with the TV on, listening to all the reporting being transmitted.

I saw Ruby pull the gun on the suspected killer. That, too, was difficult to understand. How does a person carry a gun with all the security there? Anyway, the whole incident still has me questioning the investigative commission's inquiry and results.

R.M.

I was working at the Five & Ten Cents store in South Philadelphia and was in my early twenties when President John F. Kennedy was assassinated. It was Friday, November 22, 1963. One of the maintenance employees came in and told us that the president had just been shot. I felt sad, but I didn't cry. It was just like it is today in politics; some people liked John Kennedy, and others did not.

People were willing to talk about JFK at work or on the bus or anywhere. I remember getting on the bus after work that day, and it was so quiet. I felt depressed but it didn't change my life. I thought he was a good man; I just liked him.

My mom and I tried going to Washington, DC to attend Kennedy's funeral, but the traffic was backed up, and the crowd was so enormous, so we turned back and headed home. My mom was sixty years old at the time, and the crowd was too much for her.

Donald E. Flansburg – Retired Chemistry Teacher
Buffalo, NY

I was a full-time student at SUNY Buffalo State Teachers College. At the same time, I was also a full-time employee on duty in the Fire Department - Engine 19 at Forest and Grant in Buffalo, NY when I heard shocking news on television that John F. Kennedy, our 35th president had just been shot in Dallas, Texas. I remember telling the Fire Chief, who was struck in awe by the tragic news.. He and the other three firemen, and I, congregated together to watch the news as it unfolded. Alarmed and confused, we wondered in dismay, now what?

Before leaving the Fire Department for the day, we learned that President Kennedy had been pronounced dead at one o'clock p.m. Central Standard Time.

Upon arriving home that day, I continued watching the news coverage on television and learning more about the details and the events that occurred that day and, in fact, throughout the next week.

T.D.

I was serving in the United States Navy stationed on the Mediterranean Sea at the time when I first learned about the assassination of John Fitzgerald Kennedy, President of our great county. It was already late evening as we were probably several hours ahead of Dallas, Texas, Standard Mountain Time. The staff announced the news to us over the intercom system.

At sunrise the next morning, we flew the flag at half-staff and followed orders according to Emergency Alert status. The sailors knew that Kennedy gave good orders and promoted a strong military. They weren't worried about anything.

JFK was a fine president. I felt the same painful loss when Martin Luther King, Jr. was slain. When I came home on leave from the United States Navy, my grandma was crying. The first topic of conversation she came up with was that of Kennedy's assassination. I respected him and took a drink of Scotch for him!

Elizabeth Green – Retired Medical Transcriptionist
Buffalo, NY

When President John F. Kennedy was assassinated, I was living in Buffalo, New York in an apartment house owned by my maternal grandparents, who were occupants there as well. I was expecting my first child, and working part-time, but was home on that tragic historic day.

My husband was at work. I was not tuned into my radio or TV when the news broke, but apparently my grandmother was, as she was quick to knock on my door asking if I heard the news that "the president had been shot". I immediately turned on my black & white portable TV and was glued to it the rest of the day. For the next several days, everyone I knew had their TV on, and for the first time ever, it seemed we were all watching the same thing.

Initially, I felt somewhat in a state of disbelief or denial.   I was young and only knew of such rare tragic events in history books. I thought things like that used to happen, but not in this day and age!   This was the era of Camelot! But reality soon hit, when TV anchor, Walter Cronkite solemnly announced, "The president is dead." How could this be, I wondered!

During the days that followed, I sensed a dark cloud of quiet sadness over the nation, as it seemed everyone was in mourning.

We spent the weekend visiting my parents in Dunkirk, New York. I recall my dad did not readily accept the lone assassin view at that time. He felt we did not know everything, and that the truth would eventually be uncovered and confirmed years later when it would no longer seem so vitally important.   He was greatly interested in viewing film footage of the assassination and what transpired over the next few days via uninterrupted TV news coverage and which, as I recall, overrode most scheduled programming.

Janet J. Stevenson – Retired – Fort Worth, TX

The state flag of Texas was designed with a blue vertical rectangle along the left edge and a single white lone star in the middle, a white horizontal rectangle across the top, and a red horizontal rectangle across the bottom. The flag was adopted when Texas became a state in 1845. The red represents bravery, white purity and blue loyalty.

My family was originally from Dallas, Texas, but had moved to Fort Worth, Texas in 1957 and was residing there when President Kennedy was shot. I was a freshman in college and had gone home for the weekend. I was visiting with my mother who was preparing lunch in the kitchen for my father and us when suddenly we heard a pounding at the front door which I had inadvertently locked. I ran to open it for my father who was panic stricken and crying out, "The president has been shot!"

We quickly turned on the television and stared in shock and disbelief as we tried to take in the news. As the story unfolded and we learned of the president's death, the condition of Governor Connolly, and the horrifying footage of Jackie Kennedy reaching for help, a sense of despair settled in.

On Sunday morning, I turned on the television about eleven o'clock and was watching as Lee Harvey Oswald was being transferred from Dallas City jail to the Dallas County jail when to my complete horror Jack Ruby stepped out of the crowd and shot Oswald and killed him. My parents returned home from church to find me overwhelmed by the events of the past two days.

After all these years, that weekend still stands out clearly in my memory from the assassination to the swearing in of President Johnson and later to the funeral of President Kennedy. I still recall the grief and uncertainty our country experienced following that tragic event. As a Texan, I felt a deep sense of sorrow and shame that this had happened in my beloved hometown and state.

Donna Robinson – Retired High-School Secretary – Towson, MD

Donna's Son Holding Historic Newspaper

At the time of President Kennedy's assassination in November of 1963, I was living in Towson, Maryland. I was 25 years old, and I was a maternity patient at Women's Hospital in Baltimore, MD.

On November 19th, I had just given birth of my son, Craig. Back then, a hospital stay of about five days was customary for maternity patients. I had heard that on November 22nd, President Kennedy would be going to Dallas, Texas to prepare for his re-election the following year. On that day, he would also be riding in a motorcade that would take him downtown through the streets of Dallas.

At about 1:30 p.m. on November 22nd, I saw one of the nurses running down the hall crying that the President had just been shot. In the maternity ward, the only source of outside news was a radio located at the nurses' station.

Consequently, we were not hearing further details, but it seemed that in no time at all, one of the doctors began visiting each room, announcing that the President had died. I was shocked and upset by what had happened.

The next day, I was discharged from the hospital, and on the way home, my husband stopped to pick up a newspaper to read about what had actually happened in Dallas. I kept this newspaper all these years and just recently gave it to my son. I told him to keep it as a reminder of this tragic event in American history!

Gayle Cranford – Retired – Sharon, PA

I was a young 28-year-old mother of my first child that day in November, 1963.

Having set up my ironing board in the living room in front of the TV console, I was tending to the chore of ironing my husband's business shirts. Since our child's birth, as usual, he was away selling steel pipes in Cleveland in his new job as a salesman for a small manufacturing company in western Pennsylvania, where we rented a small duplex.

I had placed my year-old daughter in her highchair beside me at the ironing board. While she contentedly played and snacked on Cheerios in her chair, I ironed, distracted by a continuing soap opera saga to which I was somewhat addicted.

Suddenly, there was a TV news alert that the President of the United States had been shot. I watched with horror as the news progressed from President Kennedy being shot in Dallas, Texas to his having been rushed to Parkland Memorial Hospital, to his eventual succumbing to those awful gunshot wounds and to his lying in state and finally, the funeral.

Shockingly, the young, attractive, intelligent John Fitzgerald Kennedy was pronounced dead. As the terrible realization of his being gone settled in and subsequent questions about the perpetrator were dramatized, I was glued to the TV the rest of that day and throughout the next several days. Camelot was over. I never watched another soap opera.

Mimi Benson – Brighton, NY

My husband and I lived in a politically Republican town. I had voted for Nixon but planned to vote for Kennedy in the next election. On the day of his death, I was sitting in my doctor's office in Brighton, New York when he took a phone call after which he told me that President Kennedy had been shot.

I left the office and drove toward home on a country road, Westfall Road as I recall, listening to the car radio. "President Kennedy is dead," a voice said, and I drove to the side of the road and stopped and just sat there.

My husband Sam and I were expecting three couples for dinner that night, and I needed dessert. So, I continued to drive on to the bakery. It was so normal in there. Women were taking turns at the counter buying bread, chatting with the baker, who in the early morning hours, had made it. They haven't heard—I thought. They don't know. I thought about telling everyone. I really wanted to. This was such an innocent scene, so ordinary, so life as usual, and our president was dead. But I didn't. I bought a cake and went home.

I remember that evening as somewhat subdued but not mournful. I think I could put into words what our guests may have thought—I didn't vote for him, but this is a tragedy. Something like that. As for me, it was probably harder. I had just changed direction politically, and this was more personal.

I wonder what it would have been like if I had had the courage to tell the women and the bread man about the tragedy. And, if one of them had been asked to write about his or her experience on the day President Kennedy died, she would write—I'll never forget it; I was standing in line in the bakery when a woman came in all upset and told all of us the president has been assassinated.

Diane Winiecki – Washington, DC

Diane Reflects on the Future of America After the Loss of President Kennedy

In the spring of 1959, I became engaged to someone who had already made up his mind to vote for John F. Kennedy if he was nominated. It was an easy choice for him as he was a Southie from Boston, and a doctoral candidate from Harvard. I, on the other hand, was convinced that Congress needed a president who could work both sides of the aisle and my choice became Lyndon Johnson. Little did we realize that eventually both our choices would be realized.

I did not marry the Southie from Boston but rather the son of a German-Polish coal miner who had inherited his father's antipathy towards the "privileged" classes or otherwise known as "elites."

My husband and I were living in Washington, DC when Kennedy was shot. Since I did not yet have my driver's license, I had to wait until his mother came to the United States for a chance to participate in Kennedy's assassination activities. My sister-in-law, my husband's own sister, took their mother to the Capitol in Washington where Kennedy lay in state. She was an elderly lady at the time yet she was proud to say she waited her turn to view a gentleman, who though not her president, she joined millions around the world to mourn his passing.

Two months later, when it was my turn to entertain my mother-in-law, a neighbor kindly offered to drive us to Arlington National Cemetery, and my husband's mother was proud to say when back in home in Germany that she had also visited John F. Kennedy's final resting place. And I was there with her to acknowledge a president who is still missed to this very day.

Kathleen Powers – Retired Secretary
SUNY Maritimes College

I was living in an apartment at 196th Street in Washington Heights, NY (borough of Manhattan) near Fort Tryon Park with my husband and two small children. Michael was a year and a half, and Kathy was ten months old, better known as Irish twins. I often enjoyed taking them outdoors for a ride in the baby carriage.

After getting them dressed on this particular day in November 1963, I trudged down four flights of stairs to the sidewalk carrying one and taking the other by the hand. I was young and energetic and enjoyed getting them out for a walk through the neighborhood and talking with those we met along the way. Usually, there wasn't much to chat about except the weather and how we were all doing.

But on this particular day, we overheard a lot of excitement in the voices of a crowd of pedestrians gathered at the corner. Others had gathered around and stopped to listen and inquire, and I, of course, did the same. I was shocked to learn that our president had been shot in Dallas, Texas. Everyone on the corner was stunned and frantic, but details were yet unknown.

So I turned around and headed back to the apartment. After climbing four flights of stairs with two small children, I turned on the TV and soon learned that the gunshot wounds were fatal and had taken the life of our president. I felt sick when I heard all the details and watched replays of the actual shooting. Most vivid in my mind, I can still see the president slumped over in the arms of Jacqueline, wife and first lady.

I'll never forget little John-John raising his right hand and saluting the casket while standing on the steps of St. Matthew's Cathedral in Washington, DC.

V.M. – Retired State Employee – Gowanda, NY

It was Friday, November 22, 1963. I was working in the cafeteria at Gowanda Psychiatric Center in Gowanda, NY. As usual, the patients seemed to be enjoying lunch. I recall the food was excellent. Most of the patients were just elderlies in need of a place to live as there were no nursing homes like we have today, and it was just like any other ordinary day until now.

About one o'clock, a patient who had been watching television in the atrium, rushed into the cafeteria to inform me of the news that President Kennedy had been shot. Of course, I wanted to know all the details surrounding this tragic event, but she had none, except that it happened in Dallas.

When I got home from work later that afternoon, I turned on the television to find out who would want to assassinate the President of the United States and why! Shortly afterward, my daughter, a fourth grader arrived home from school only to see me crying. I tried to explain what had happened and how awful I felt about it. Being so young and trying to comfort me, she said, "But you didn't know him."

Most vivid in my memory of that tragic day was seeing Jackie Kennedy still clothed in the same blood-stained outfit, as she stood on Air Force One before takeoff while Vice-President Lyndon B. Johnson was sworn in to office. The expression of sadness on her face told me her world had crashed!

Barbara O'Shea – Retired Teacher – Binghamton, NY

Barbara and Tom on the Campaign Trail

Who can forget that dreadful day President Kennedy was assassinated? I was teaching third grade at St. John the Evangelist Elementary School in Binghamton, New York. Suddenly, our principal Sister Raymond turned on the public address system, and in her characteristically low-keyed, soft-spoken manner told us that the President of the United States had just been shot in Dallas, Texas. Shock swept through the building like a bolt of lightning. Sister Raymond immediately asked the entire faculty and student body to join her in prayer.

When school was dismissed, I walked a short distance home and waited for my husband. I figured he might be late because the male faculty always played basketball in the gym after school on Fridays. And so – they did today, as well. Fully aware of the tragic events of the day, I realized it was probably more therapeutic for him "working out" than it would have been otherwise.

I married into an Irish family and now lived in an Irish community. I was Catholic and had voted for President Kennedy, but I was not Irish. During this week, however, I was immersed in Irish culture, values, and learned a great deal about the entire Kennedy family from those around me. I remember how they marveled especially about the president's mother, Rose Kennedy. I had been indoctrinated in a very short period of time.

We watched continuous coverage on the news channels and witnessed history in the making that weekend and throughout the following week—learning first-hand about the assassination, about widows and orphans coping with grief, transfer of power, the wake at the U.S. Capitol Rotunda, and burial at Arlington Cemetery, etc. Although schools, colleges, and universities were closed the following week, I would venture to say we all acquired enormous awareness and deeper insight into the life and loss of a great American president—John Fitzgerald Kennedy, unfortunately, however, at a price we could not afford to pay.

William R. Parks – Math & Computer Science Teacher – 1960 to 1997. Currently – Semi-Retired Book Publisher. Web site: www.wrparks.com

Bill and Judy Parks on their honeymoon in the year 1963 when President Kennedy was assassinated

In 1963 I was in my second year teaching math and science subjects at a Catholic high school in Western New York State. In the afternoon I had a free period and sat in an office to take incoming phone calls.

I was teaching in a separate building from the main campus where some of the classes were taught. I got a call from the main campus and was told that TV national news was reporting that President Kennedy had been shot in Dallas, Texas and had died. I decided to inform each classroom teacher.

First, I knocked on the door of the English teacher, a lay teacher like myself, and told her the sad news. She became very distraught and sad and said nothing except an exclamation and closed the door.

Next, I went to a priest's classroom where he was teaching economics. I knocked on his classroom door and he stepped into the hallway with me. I quietly told him what had just happened in Dallas, Texas and he said, "We do not want to cause panic. Let's wait for more information before we tell the students." He closed the door and went back to teaching.

Then I walked across the hall to a nun's religion class and knocked on her door and told her the sad news. She made a brief, sad exclamation, closed the door and before I had a chance to leave, the sister asked her entire class to pray and I heard them praying out loud.

Finally, I went to the foreign language class taught by a recent immigrant teacher. I knocked on his door and he stepped into the hallway. I gave him the sad news but he reacted differently than the others. He proceeded to criticize me for interrupting his class lecture and then he left me standing in the hallway as he briskly closed the door.

I went back to the office and phoned my wife Judy to tell her the sad news and she turned on our home TV set.

Audrey Seidel – Retired Teacher – Buffalo, NY

Audrey Seidel decorating Christmas tree with neighbor's children while serving in the Peace Corp in Columbia, South America.

Jacqueline Kennedy and Family Visit JFK Grave Circa 1965

My mother wasn't feeling well, so I picked up the phone to call a doctor. As I dialed the number, the operator said, "There is a national emergency! No calls can be connected." So we turned on the television and heard that President John F. Kennedy had been shot.

I had campaigned for Kennedy in my freshman year of college even though I was not old enough yet to vote in a presidential election. I was only eighteen, and at that time, the required voting age was twenty-one.

My sister called hysterically for me to come and pick her up at the University of Buffalo where she was a student. Upon returning home, we watched the news, in fact, all weekend long.

In January 1964, my sister, her friend, and I took the train to Washington, DC to visit Kennedy's grave. At that time, it was decorated with a simple eternal flame and white picket fence.

In 1965, I joined the Peace Corps and was stationed in Columbia, South America for two years. I was inspired by President Kennedy who founded the Peace Corps. I am currently serving on the board of the Returned Peace Corps Volunteers in Buffalo, New York.

Thomas McArdle – Former IBMer & Retired Business Owner

In November 1963, one of my IBM accounts was American Chicle Co. in Long Island City (borough of Queens), New York.

On the day of the assassination of President John Fitzgerald Kennedy, we had planned to meet with a Chinese fellow who, as I recall, was either a consultant for a large firm (Peat Marwick, Arthur Anderson?) or a member of the firm we would all meet with later that day at the Warner Lambert office in New Jersey. The group included the Treasurer of American Chicle, their Data Processing Manager, the Chinese consultant, and of course, me.

On the road trip by car down to Warner Lambert, we were discussing some of the applications that were being performed on their punch card equipment and some of their thinking. I believe, but memory is clouded, that we were planning to upgrade their present punch card calculator to the newer 609 Calculator. I believe the consultant was there to see how the data processing side of the business fit in with what they were doing at Warner Lambert.

Have not researched this, but I think American Chicle Company later became part of Warner Lambert. One of American Chicle 's products was Rolaids which over the years has been quite popular.

Suddenly, in the middle of our discussion, we were interrupted by an important but brief news bulletin on the car radio. The president of the United States had just been shot in Dallas, Texas during a motor parade. Details were not yet available. It was probably around noontime when we heard it on the car radio, and, as you can imagine, the "product talk" was interrupted, as well. The business discussion the four of us were having at the time pretty much ceased altogether.

Upon arriving at Warner Lambert in New Jersey for our scheduled meeting, we met with the others as planned. After a robust sharing of details regarding the shooting, of course, trying to learn more about the fate of our president, the meeting was called to order, and it was business as usual. The Chinese consultant listened to our discussion between the groups, and the Warner Lambert crowd took notes. The meeting was adjourned, and we all headed home for the weekend.

J.H.B. – Student at Dunkirk High School
Dunkirk, NY

I was taking a test in my physics class at Dunkirk High School, Dunkirk, N.Y., when a woman knocked on the door. The teacher stepped into the hall briefly to talk to her, then returned and made the following announcement to the class: "That was my wife. She stopped to say that she heard on the car radio that the President and the Governor of Texas were shot. One was shot in the head and the other was shot in the stomach, but she wasn't sure which was which." We then continued with the Physics test. That was the final class of the day.

When we got to our home rooms, the public address system came on carrying a live feed from a Buffalo radio station that had a national network affiliation. While we were still in our home rooms, the official announcement came over the air that President Kennedy was dead. At that moment, my home room teacher, a youthful, athletic man who rarely displayed emotions, collapsed into the nearest chair at one of the students' desks, tears rolling down his cheeks.

This was dismissal time, which was usually a noisy time of the day with much loud chattering and the slamming of locker doors as the kids got their coats to go home, but this day everyone was very subdued. There was only a little quiet talk among the students. Even the sounds of the locker doors seemed subdued, maybe so that we could hear what was being said over the radio feed that was still coming through the p.a. system.

When I got home, which was just across the street, my mother was watching the events on TV and, over the weekend, my experiences were the same as those of millions of other Americans who had gathered around their sets to watch the events unfold. Those events included what is probably still the most widely witnessed murder in history, the shooting of the accused Kennedy assassin, Lee Harvey Oswald, by nightclub owner Jack Ruby on live television while he was in police custody.

Jill O'Hara – Freelance Writer

I was eight years old, a third grader in Mrs. Belvin's class at Franklin Elementary School in Okmulgee, Oklahoma. As I waited in line with the other children to go to recess, Mr. Johnson, school principal, stopped by our classroom and said something to Mrs. Belvin, who was standing just inside the doorway.

I was near the back of the line, chattering as usual and completely oblivious to the principal's mumbling.

I was startled when Kenneth, the boy in front of me, turned around, looked at me sternly and said, "Shhh. Be quiet! President Kennedy's been shot."

Startled at being scolded by a mere classmate, I decided that this must have been some sort of joke, and simply responded, 'Oh, no he isn't'. After all, things like that just didn't happen in this great country of ours.

The rest of the school day seemed to go on as usual. Although the teachers most likely talked among themselves, I do not recall them discussing the terrible tragedy with us or asking us how we felt about it, as would counselors and teachers nowadays. Perhaps they were cautiously hopeful that he would miraculously recover. Maybe they were just too stunned to say anything.

Kenneth's words about the president were confirmed when I skipped home after school, ran to the den and flipped on the TV to watch my favorite after-school programs. What I encountered on virtually every channel was the same coverage of absolute chaos, narrated by the matchless voice of Walter Cronkite.

My parents seemed determined to keep things calm around the house for the sake of my sister and me. Although they were not supporters of Kennedy, I do remember the sorrowful tones of discussions at the dinner table that week.

My mother seemed especially concerned and saddened about President Kennedy's children and remembered reading that, prior to the tragedy, Jackie Kennedy had been working on birthday party plans for Caroline and John Jr.

From my own eight-year old perspective I was caught up in my own immature desire for things to return to normal. Each day after school since that fateful day, I would come home, turn on the TV, hoping to see the familiar characters of my favorite programs again. The surreal nature of the events that had taken place in our nation played out in news coverage the same way day after day for what seemed like an eternity.

I watched the same funeral procession, listened to the same dirge, looked at the same American flag draped over our President's coffin as it slowly made its way through the streets of Washington, over and over again.

Then one day, I realized that things would never be the same.

Barbara Woodworth – Journalist – Buffalo, NY

**Barbara with her husband, Dr. William Woodworth,
and their two children**

There are not many instances in life that one can specifically recall knowing where one was at a particular date or time. For me, November 22, 1963 was not the case. Today the devastating events of that day remain as vivid as though they occurred yesterday.

On November 22, 1963 I was home with my one year-old twins. Having been to my GYN the day before I knew things were not going well for my current pregnancy. Told to rest, I settled my twins and their toys on the floor next to me while I reclined on the couch, as per doctors' orders.

My husband, then a fifth-grade teacher, was at school and I was sorely looking forward to him coming home as soon as the workday ended.

Not expecting any daytime phone calls, I was surprised when the phone rang. Slowly I rose to answer our one household phone, several steps away in the kitchen. The call was from my husband, who after presenting the sad news to his students, wanted to relay the terrible news of the President's passing to me rather than having me shocked by hearing the news on television.

Needless to say I was distraught. My husband and I were Kennedy supporters. In fact, we stayed up late into the night to listen to the results on the radio on election night. The outcome that night was good – this was not.

The news was horrible, horrific, appalling. Our country was in mourning, as was I. I cried most of the day as I watched the news unfold on TV. That night things got worse. I started to hemorrhage and as soon as my husband arranged for a babysitter for our twins, we left for the hospital. For me and my husband, November 22, 1963 will always be a reminder of the loss of two lives – our country's president and the baby we lost.

Sally Crosiar -- Waltham Grade School
Utica, IL

Somewhere in the 1980's, I attended a professional seminar about the importance of childhood events on our eventual development. I was told, "What you are now is where you were then." The theory – first proposed by Morris Massey – was that what happened at age ten predicted who you'd become.

In 1963 I was ten years old. Our principal interrupted Mrs. Malone's fifth grade class. "The president has been shot!" Mrs. Malone shifted seamlessly from diagramming sentences into Civics 101.

"We don't know how bad it is," she said. "But if President Kennedy dies, who will become our new president?"

"The Vice President!" all but the dimmest replied. We'd had two years of social studies by then.

"And the Vice President is?" asked Mrs. Malone. Not one of us knew. We called out names we'd heard as our parents listened to the news. "Dirksen?" No. He was our Senator from Illinois. "Nixon?" No. He lost the election to President Kennedy. "Dean Rusk?" No.

Mrs. Malone was getting impatient. She was well known as the strictest teacher in our small school, so all of us got nervous. She seemed disappointed too – and that pushed us harder. I guessed, "Henry Cabot Lodge?"

Mrs. Malone wrinkled her brow. "He died years ago. How did you come up with him?

My face probably went red. "I think the Vice President's name starts with an 'I'?"

I don't remember another time when Mrs. Malone gave partial credit. Since we knew nothing about him, we gained little wisdom hearing the name, Lyndon Baines Johnson. After a few days glued to our black and white televisions, we knew more.

Of the three hundred sixty-five days I was ten years old, few moments stand out so clearly as blurting Henry Cabot Lodge or returning home after church Sunday morning to hear Uncle Dudley's announcement that Ruby shot Lee Harvey Oswald.

What I am now is where I was then? I'm not entirely convinced, except for two things. I have and will always pay more attention to our Vice President. And I will always diagram sentences in my head before I commit them to paper just in case I meet Mrs. Malone in the after-life. I wouldn't want to risk disappointing her again.

Deborah F. Simon – Kenmore, NY

Presenting my pass, I climbed the three steps and found a seat on the bus. It was nearly empty and eerily quiet. I sat alone and stared silently at the old man across the aisle who sobbed soundlessly. Removing his glasses, he wiped his eyes with the moist handkerchief he held in his hand. I had never seen a grown man cry before. I was 14 years old.

The President had been shot. We had watched it over and over again in the auditorium while we waited to be dismissed. I only knew this man, this President, as a small figure who came to us in black and white and greys, like Ed Sullivan. Now, suddenly in death he seemed more alive.

Our television was on when I arrived home— usually unheard of in our house until after homework and dinner. We watched the news. Walter Cronkite removed his glasses one more time and wiped his eyes as he spoke, "The president is dead," struggling with the tears that overflowed with sadness. I cried.

Carolyn Takach – Retired Executive Assistant

Remembering JFK Assassination – Red Grapes

It was lunch time and the office of Right of Way and Claims at the New York Telephone Company in Buffalo, NY was almost empty. I was hurriedly typing a Right of Way document for an agent on his way to meet with a customer. Their signature would allow us to install a telephone pole on their property. I was annoyed because that made me late for lunch.

Suddenly one of the other agents shouted that the president was shot in Texas and turned up the volume on our little, cream-colored, office radio. We continued to work but with an ear to breaking news reports. We expected to hear that, though wounded, he would recover.

I was sitting at the back of the office half done with my lunch when the shocking announcement was made that President John F. Kennedy had died. Everyone stopped what they were doing and we stood and looked at each other like a bunch of zombies. Tears came to our eyes, followed by fear and dozens of questions. What will happen to our country now and how, why and who. The office became eerily quiet. The president of America had been assassinated. This was an historic moment. I daresay this scenario played out in thousands of offices that day.

In the week that followed, it was difficult to concentrate on anything and we all hurried home every day to watch the news reports on TV.

Who was Oswald and why did Jack Ruby kill him; the rotunda, the long lines of mourners, the replaying of the fatal shots with Jackie Kennedy crawling to the top of the back seat of the convertible. It was a very emotional and sad time. Regardless of political affiliation the country mourned as one.

Many businesses and offices were closed the day of the funeral.

My husband and I sat on the couch and gloomily watched the cortege: the riderless, white horse with one black boot facing backward in the stirrup, signifying the rider was dead; little Jon-Jon waving the small flag; so many leaders from every country in the world; so many people in the streets all paying respect.

The emotional stress, fear and sadness of those days affected me a lot. I was 24, four months pregnant, had morning sickness at any time of the day and felt miserable most days. The day of the funeral I ate red grapes while watching TV. I had been feeling nauseated all along and immediately after seeing the rider less horse, I ran to the bathroom to regurgitate. To this day I do not eat red grapes. Even seeing them in stores and markets brings an immediate flashback to the events of that horrible week, especially the riderless horse. That image is seared into my memory. Red grapes are a connection to that memory which I will never forget. The day JFK died, our world changed. We are no longer a nation of innocent, trusting people.

Helene Lee – Library Technician – Cheektowaga, NY

I remember that fateful day very well. I was living in Cheektowaga, NY. I stood at the ironing board pressing my husband's dress shirts that he wore daily to Cornell Lab along with tie and creased pants. Since I considered ironing boring I set up the board in the dining room so I could watch TV and keep an eye on my 4-year-old daughter playing nearby. My older daughter and son were in elementary school.

The last week of November was not a good time for us. Yes, the children were excited about upcoming Christmas, but I already had sad memories of this time of year. My 21-month-old little girl died of leukemia the previous November on the 22nd. These memories flooded through me. In later years, I would add my husband's and my father's deaths in November.

I remember shivering when I heard about the president's death. That day, I worried that this heinous act could be the catalyst for another world war. I recalled the Bay of Pigs action and the Russian's establishing missile bases in nearby Cuba. Were they responsible for this infamous killing? So much to consider, so many fears like would my husband and friends be recalled into Service? I believe all our Armed Forces went on High Alert that day. I recall many phone calls to my husband, family; then phones tied up. I remember scooping up my daughter, holding her close, protecting her from the unknown, absorbing her warmth to calm my shivering as we watched television.

And I shed tears for Jackie and her children. My husband and I tried to explain this horrible act to our children, and so I wondered how Jackie told her young daughter and son. I admired her fortitude throughout the entire ordeal and prayed for them, for our country, and my family. Every year when November comes along, memories somewhat suppressed become real again.

Robert Hill – Retired GM cutter/grinder
Tonawanda, NY

I was shopping at Murphy's 5 & 10 Cents Store in Tonawanda, New York for a variety of small household items when I heard President John F. Kennedy was assassinated. My wife and I were looking over merchandise when suddenly over the loud speaker a store employee let us know that our president had been shot. It was shocking news that worked everyone up.

My wife and I decided to leave the store and head home to check on our children. It was hard explaining to them what was happening. They didn't understand, and we tried to keep things as normal as possible for them. We listened to the radio almost constantly for the following days to try and learn more about the tragedy.

John Kennedy was a good president, and this was a sad time for our country. As a United States Marine, I was touched by this senseless act and couldn't help but imagine myself in that situation. It made me think of my family and how terrible it was for the president's wife, Jacqueline to experience having him shot seated right next to her in an open convertible automobile and how tragic it was!

James Kehrer – Retired custodian
Buffalo, NY

I was a student at McKinley High School in Buffalo, New York attending my horticulture class. We were learning about the many different kind of plants, and how to care for them, and especially how to transplant small plants when ready which was all very interesting.

In the middle of explaining all of this, our teacher, Mr. Martino stopped briefly to tell us the news of our president's death. Within five minutes, he picked up where he left off in his lesson and continued teaching which surprised me. School was dismissed at the usual time of day, too, as I recall.

Of course, we were all saddened by the news. I watched TV and listened to the radio all night. The assassination of our president, John F. Kennedy made me feel bad. I felt sad for his family. This caused me to appreciate my family more, and I wanted to spend as much time with them as I could.

Rosemarie Dudek – Homemaker – Cheektowaga, NY

I remember it was a very cold and snowy day in Western New York. I was about fourteen years old at the time and a student at Cheektowaga Junior-Senior High School in Cheektowaga, New York.

I was in a good mood that day. It was Friday, November 22, 1963. Following my normal schedule at school, things were going well. I was in study hall with Miss Kaspersak, and everything seemed fine until— I heard the announcement over the public-address system. Shock and sadness caused my classmates to become upset. We were all confused and many of us couldn't hold back tears. I recall feeling confusion and a bit of fear as a I waited for the bus to pick us up. We were all sent home early.

I was hurt—who could do this to the president? Why would anyone do this? I remember being upset at home and my mother asking me, "Why are you crying? You didn't know him," as she tried comforting me.

I was the oldest of six children in my family and took care of my younger siblings while our mom went to work as a cleaning lady that evening. Therefore, I had to keep some sense of calm for my younger siblings by playing games and keeping the normal bedtime routine with stories and laughter.

Betty Hager – Retired Dictaphone Operator
Buffalo, NY

When I woke up that day I was cheerful; it was payday after all! I went to work as usual and had even planned to relax by grabbing a drink after work with some friends—sadly, that would never happen. The ladies from the office and I had made it to our hour-long lunch, and decided we would cash our checks and get lunch at the sit-down restaurant close to our Ellicott Square office building in downtown Buffalo.

We had finished ordering our lunch when we heard a blood-curdling scream from the restaurant's cook. In a confused and shocked panic, we turned on the tv and with the other patrons we learned of the terrible news. "Nah, this can't be happening. Things like this don't happen in the United States." My mind was racing as I tried to comprehend. Disbelief turned to sadness and concern, all I could think about was my sister and her husband, a U.S. Navy Sailor. They were all the way in California and I feared that this horrible act would be putting them into danger.

The office crew and I were engrossed in the news, and our lunch break was going over its allowed hour-long period. We got our food when the cook was composed enough to continue her work.

When we arrived back to the office we were reprimanded by our supervisor for taking an extended break. She screamed at us and threatened to make us stay late to make up our time. I was shocked at her attitude in a time of such horror. The head supervisor then came out of his office, taking our supervisor aside to let her know she needed to sit and listen to the radio," JFK is dead," he said. The head of the Buffalo office apologized to us for our supervisor's inappropriate response.

It was comforting to be home that evening with my parents, my sister and her fiancé. My grandma came to stay with us, too. When we were all together I took comfort in knowing they were safe. All my previous plans for that evening would without a second thought be cancelled. I made a big casserole that night, enough to feed the family for the weekend as we were glued to the TV, trying to further understand what was happening in our country where we had previously felt so safe.

My family kept in constant contact that weekend with my sister and her husband in California. The United States Navy was on alert. That following Monday I got dressed, my usually normal schedule now feeling off. When I got to work, I waited and waited. My supervisor had never called to tell me the office was closed that day.

Charlotte Cash Lasher – Lockport, NY

Who would have guessed that November 1963 would be such a sad and historic month? I was teaching 9th grade Economic World in Williamsville Junior High School, a suburb of Buffalo, New York. My parents, Clifford and Mary Cash, were living in another suburb, the Town of Tonawanda. I had moved to Lockport N.Y., a nearby small city, after graduation from the University of Rochester. Here my husband, Keith and I, and son Craig, had moved into a new home in 1961.

My dad had suffered with heart problems for a long time, since his freshman year at Colgate University, when he contacted rheumatic fever and had to drop out of college. He was left with a defective mitral valve in his heart and suffered various bouts of pneumonia, pleurisy and other heart problems for all my youth.

In 1963, Buffalo General Hospital was in the beginning stages of open heart surgery, and my father would be one of the first. He had discussed the surgery at length with my mother. She would have to decide. The surgery was scheduled for Monday morning November 10th. On Sunday, we received a call from my mother that they had taken Dad to Buffalo General, where he died before I could get there. What a terrible and sad shock! He was only 59 years of age! – What would have happened in surgery? My mother would never have forgiven herself because of her decision for his surgery. A higher power had intervened.

The rest of the week was horrible, and I was on bereavement leave. I returned to school the following week, very sad but surviving. At the end of the week, Friday November 22nd, I was in the midst of teaching a class when the sad news came across the public-address system regarding the assassination of President Kennedy. From that point on we tried to continue while we waited for further news. Hope prevailed until the final announcement that our president had died. Another terrible and sad shock!

In November 1963 I had lost my father and the Father of my Country, the President of the United States, John F. Kennedy.

APPENDIX

WARNINGS Concerning Source Materials

by Arthur Parks

Over the past half-century thousands of books, articles, radio and television programs and movies have weighed in on the JFK assassination.

As Gerald Posner in his brilliantly researched book, *Case Closed*, warns us in his preface:

1) "As in every famous case, people have come out of the woodwork for their fifteen minutes of fame."

2) "The only casualty is truth, especially in a society where far too many people are content to receive all their knowledge on an important issue from a single article or a three-hour movie."

3) "…the JFK murder has, regrettably, become an entertainment business, complete with board games and shopping mall "assassination research centers" stuffed with souvenir t-shirts and bumper stickers."

I recommend Gerald Posner's outstanding book, *Case Closed*, without any reservations. It was published by Random House in 1993 and consists of the following: a total of 608 pages, 16 pages of photographs, 7 pages of bibliography and an astounding 70 pages of footnotes which reinforce the historical integrity of *Case Closed*!

Another excellent book is *John F. Kennedy* by Alan Brinkley. This is a modest book of less than 200 pages, but contains six pages of bibliography, 23 pages of footnotes and is one of the books in The *American Presidents Series*, which was edited by the distinguished historian, Arthur M. Schlesinger Jr. and Sean Wilentz. Henry Holt & Company of *Time Books* published it.

Both books that I recommend contain the listings of hundreds of sources such as the *Warren Commission Report*.

NOTES

Zapruder film Zoomed in plus SUPER SLOW MOTION (HIGH QUALITY)

https://www.youtube.com/watch?v=eqzJQE8LYrQ

JFK Assassination Magic Bullet Computer Recreation

https://www.youtube.com/watch?v=PfSXkfV_mhA

Zapruder Film Slow Motion (HIGHER QUALITY)

https://www.youtube.com/watch?v=iU83R7rpXQY

JFK Assassination Zapruder Film Digitally Remastered

https://www.youtube.com/results?search_query=JFK+
Assassination+Zapruder+Film+Digitally+Remastered+

ABOUT THE AUTHORS

Barbara O'Shea

Barbara O'Shea was born and raised in Dunkirk, NY situated along the shores of Lake Erie. She earned a B.A. degree in Education from the State University of New York (SUNY/Fredonia) and an M.S. degree from Niagara University.

Barbara began her teaching career in Binghamton, NY where she taught third grade for five years. Her husband accepted a position as principal in the Northern Tioga School District, Elkland, PA and the family moved across the state line where they resided for three years, and Barbara also accepted a position in Pennsylvania as a reading teacher.

The family returned to New York State after three years when her husband accepted a position as principal in the Lockport School System. Barbara continued her career in teaching. She was hired at Lewiston-Porter School District where she taught twenty-four years before retiring.

She is a member of the NYSRTA (New York State Retired Teachers Association), ENCRTA (Eastern Niagara Co. Retired Teachers Association), NYSUT (New York State United Teachers), PGSNYS (Polish Genealogical Society of New York State), and has enjoyed searching her roots at ancestry.com for many years.

As a member of Buffalo-based POMOST International, Barbara traveled to Poland in the summer of 2010 where she taught conversational English. She also enjoys writing and has published a children's picture book, titled *Dziadek's Job*.

William R. Parks

Bill Parks was also born and raised in Dunkirk. NY in a home next door to Barbara O'Shea. He earned a B.S. degree in Mathematics from Indiana Institute of Technology, M.S. from Canisius College, and an Ed.M. from SUNY/Buffalo.

He was curriculum designer for computer science degree programs at three colleges in the SUNY system and was instructor of mathematics and computer courses at three high schools, three community colleges and four four-year colleges. He taught at SUNY colleges in Fredonia and Buffalo; Niagara County Community College, NY; Cecil Community College, MD; Elon University, NC; Walters State Community College, TN; D'Youville College, NY and Mesa Community College, AZ. He was technical editor for two national publications "Personal Computing" and "PC AI" magazine.

Currently, he works part-time as a book publisher, literary agent and author of computer math books.

Phone: **(716) 810-2726**
Email: **stanwrite (at) aol.com**
Web Site: **www.wrparks.com**
Twitter: **www.twitter.com/wparkspublishing**
Facebook: **www.facebook.com/wparkspublishing**

MORE FROM WILLIAM R. PARKS

Letters to a Young Math Teacher
Revised 2nd Edition ©2015

by Dr. Gerald Rising

Five Star Review:

"An excellent book for beginning teachers, this work shows considerable insight and understanding of the real world of the schools and the daily issues and problems that new teachers will no doubt confront. It offers balanced and experienced perspective and helpful tips. I recommend this as a useful read for every new math instructor at the secondary level." - Greg A. Baugher, Mercer University, Georgia

The Joyful Cook's Guide to Heavenly Greek Cuisine

by Georget Photos

"I love the recipes in this book! Even though I work long days, I want to prepare delicious meals for my family and entertain friends. These recipes are quick and easy to make." – Dr. Maria Secaras

A Franciscan Odyssey

by Father Lucjan Krolikowski, OFM Conv.

Translated by Dr. Gosia Brykczynska

Incredible true story! Arrested by the NKVD (Soviet Secret Police) along with thousands of Polish citizens,the author, Father Łucjan Królikowski,was deported with them in box cars to Soviet labor camps. After the War he adopted 150 orphaned children whose parents had died in the Soviet labor camps.

Made in America: Sustainable Building Products, Materials & Methods - 2nd Edition

by Robert A Wozniak Jr.

As stated by Anders Lewendal, Builder and Economist: "If every builder bought just 5% more U.S. made materials, they would create 220,000 American jobs right now."

As an effort to help continue to stimulate and sustain the USA economy, this book celebrates, promotes and honors those companies that have and continue to employ the American workforce to creatively design, fabricate and distribute the various green building materials and products – proudly made and listed within.

A Book for Birdwatchers Who Wish to Go Beyond Field Identification

Hershey, PA – William R. Parks is proud to announce the publication of Gerry Rising's latest book, "Birds and Birdwatchers." Dr. Rising, a nationally recognized educator and writer, is SUNY Distinguished Teaching Professor Emeritus at the University at Buffalo.

www.ingramcontent.com/pod-product-compliance
Lightning Source LLC
Chambersburg PA
CBHW071618040426

42452CB00009B/1389